ENGLISH CHINESE

VISUAL DICTIONARY

Tuomas Kilpi

OPPIAN

Publisher: Oppian Press
Helsinki, Finland
All rights reserved
ISBN 978-951-877-145-9

Table of Contents • 目录

fork
叉
knife
刀
spoon
汤匙
plate
盘子
pot
锅
glass
水杯

frying pan
平底锅

mug
杯子

teapot
茶壶

strainer
滤网

spatula
锅铲

beans
豆子

rice
米饭

potato
土豆

date
枣

tea
茶
coffee
咖啡
apple
苹果
pear
梨
banana
香蕉

sweet potato
红薯

carrot
胡萝卜

garlic
大蒜

onion
洋葱

pineapple
菠萝

strawberry
草莓

orange
橙子

coconut
椰子

lemon
柠檬

kiwi fruit
奇异果

cucumber
黄瓜

tomato
西红柿

raspberry
覆盆子

grapes
葡萄

apricot
杏

papaya
木瓜

melon
甜瓜
plum
梅子
mango
芒果
watermelon
西瓜

aubergine
茄子

fig
无花果

chili
辣椒

cauliflower
菜花

turnip
芜菁

leek
韭葱

cabbage
卷心菜

mushroom
蘑菇

lettuce
生菜

salt
盐

flour
面粉

sugar
糖

cooking oil
食用油

margarine
人造黄油
milk
牛奶
cheese
起司
bread
面包

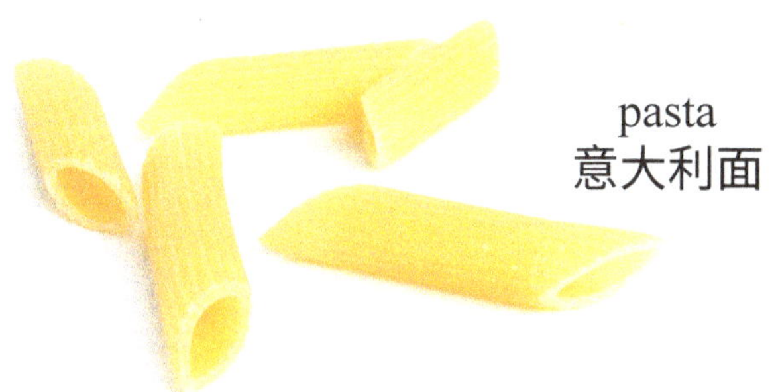

pasta
意大利面

ice cream
冰淇淋

cookie
曲奇饼

chocolate
巧克力

hamburger
汉堡包

sandwich
三明治

candy
糖果

pizza
比萨

man
男人

woman
女人

girl
女孩

boy
男孩

coat
外套

pants
裤子

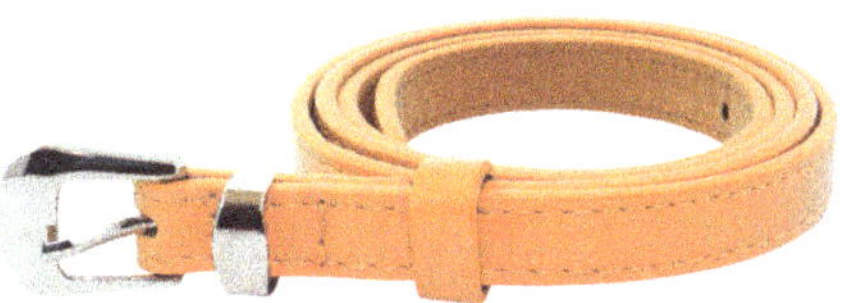

belt
腰带

socks
袜子

shoes
鞋子

T-shirt
T恤衫

skirt
裙子

scarf
围巾

boots
靴子

hat
帽子

lamb
羊
fish
鱼
cow
牛
cat
猫

pig
猪

dog
狗

chicken
鸡

egg
蛋

hare
野兔

bear
熊

squirrel
松鼠

rat
老鼠

wolf
狼

fox
狐狸

moose
驼鹿

snake
蛇

snail
蜗牛

spider
蜘蛛

frog
青蛙

wasp
黄蜂

bee
蜜蜂

fly
苍蝇

mosquito
蚊子

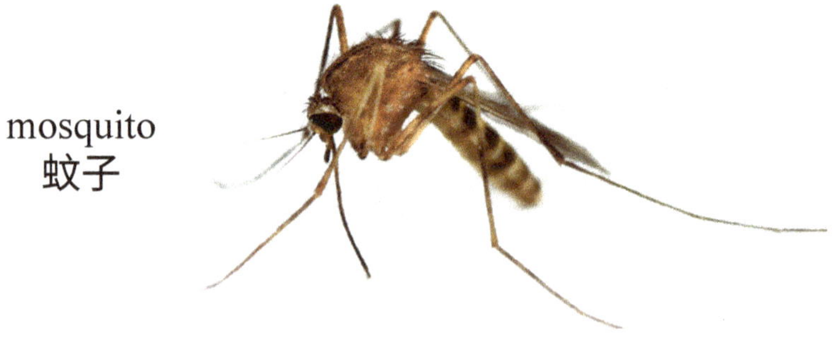

bathroom
浴室

kitchen
厨房

bedroom
卧室

living room
客厅

ceiling
天花板

window
窗户

wall
墙壁

floor
地板

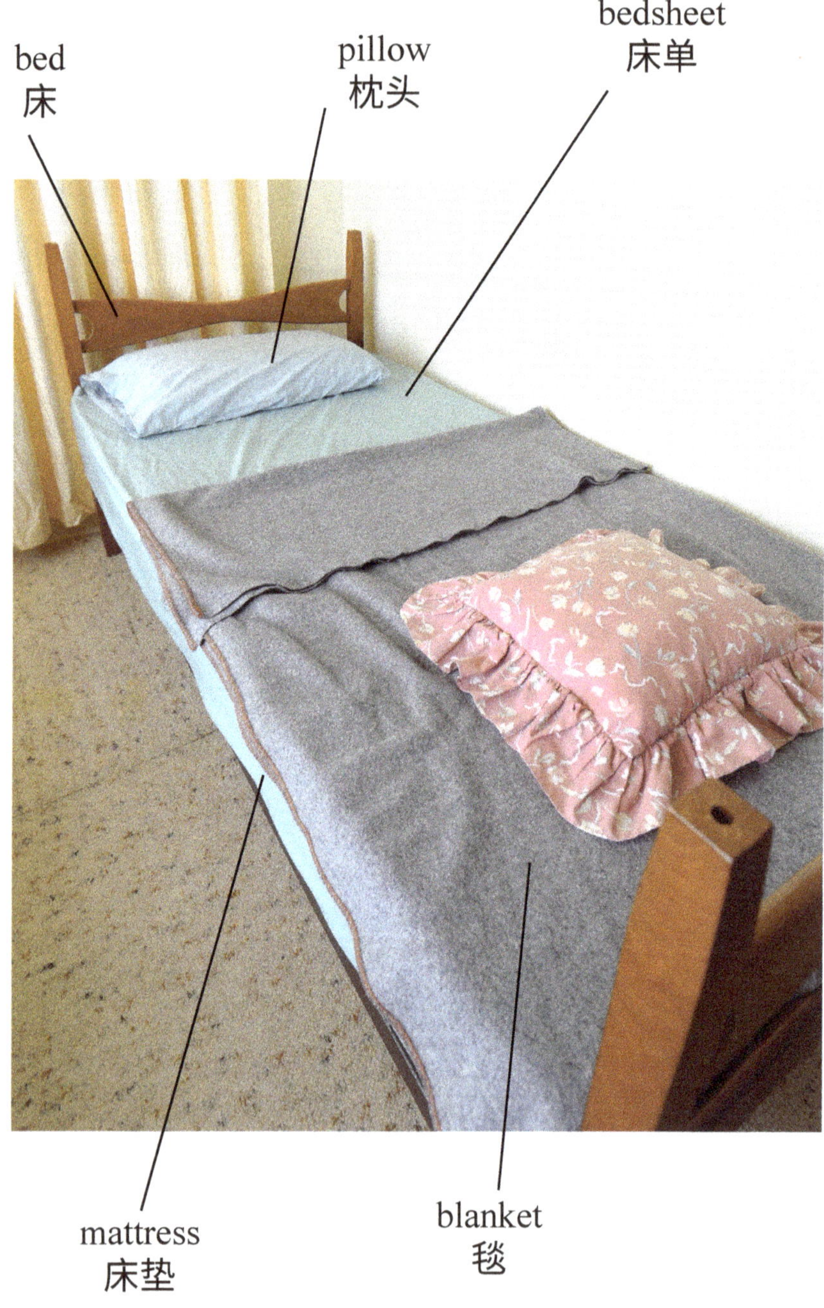

bed
床

pillow
枕头

bedsheet
床单

mattress
床垫

blanket
毯

rug
地毯

umbrella
雨伞

lamp
灯

table
桌子

chair
椅子

scissors
剪刀

envelope
信封

tape
胶带

parcel
邮包

stamp
邮票

soap
肥皂

toilet paper
卫生纸

toothbrush
牙刷

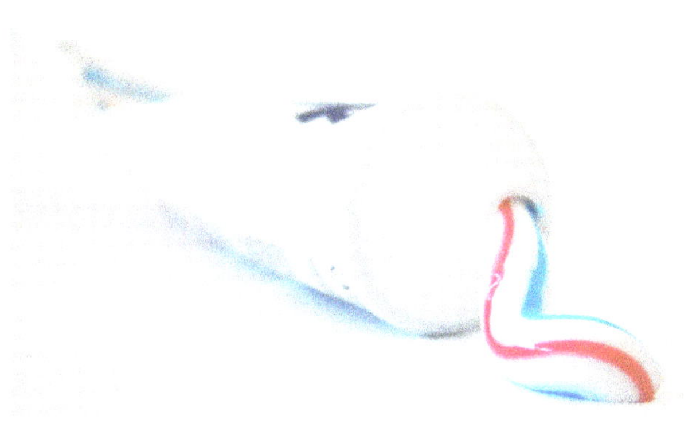

toothpaste
牙膏

brush
刷子
comb
梳子
dental floss
牙线
deodorant
止汗剂
scale
磅秤
electric razor
电动剃须刀

television
电视

remote control
遥控器

mouse
滑鼠

computer
电脑

memory stick
记忆棒

printer
打印机

charger
充电器

phone
电话

stove
炉灶

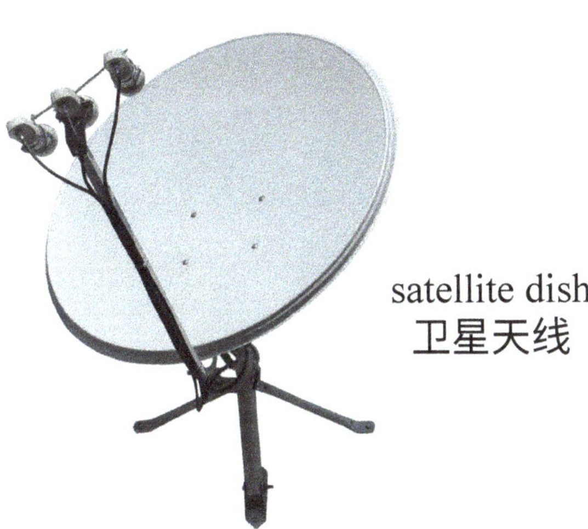

satellite dish
卫星天线

headphones
头戴式耳机

radio
收音机

book
书

map
地图

flashlight
手电筒

tape measure
卷尺
shovel
铲
rake
耙
pliers
钳
saw
锯

jar
玻璃罐

bottle
瓶子

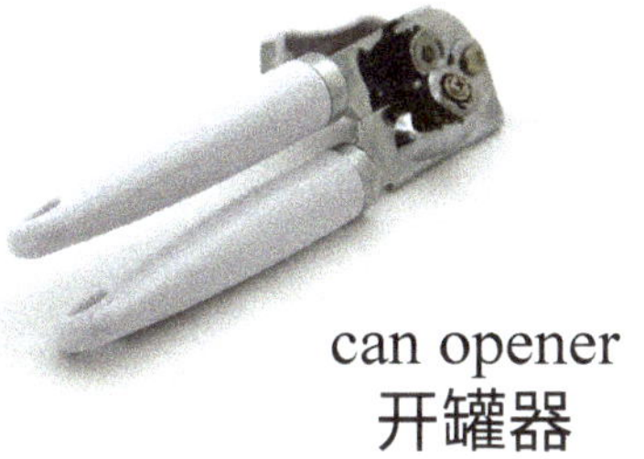

can opener
开罐器

bottle opener
开瓶器

tin can
罐头

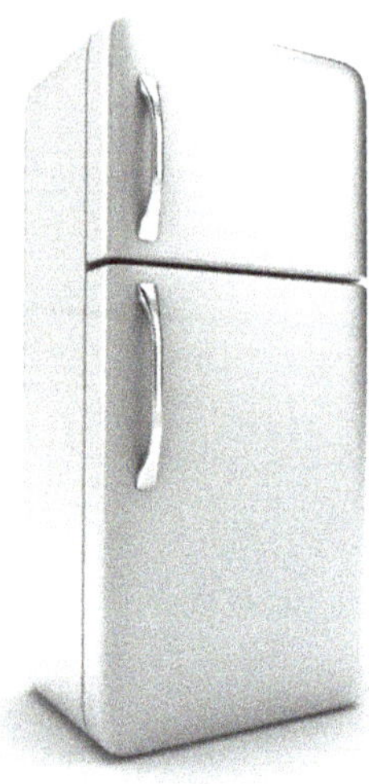

refigerator
冰箱

thread
线

needle
针

clothes peg
衣服夹子

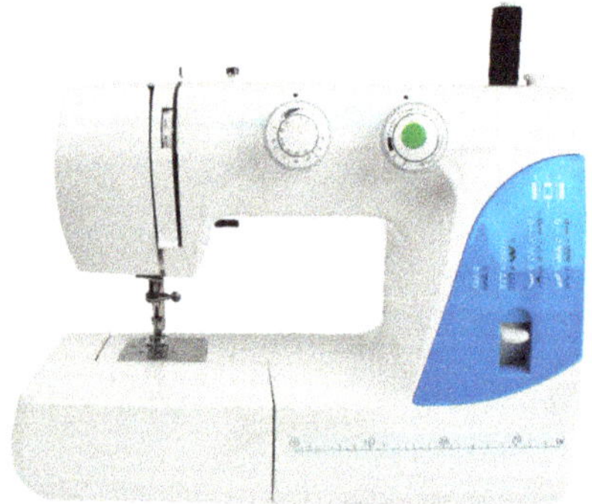

sewing machine
缝纫机

microwave oven
微波炉

key
钥匙

calculator
计算器

eyeglasses
眼镜

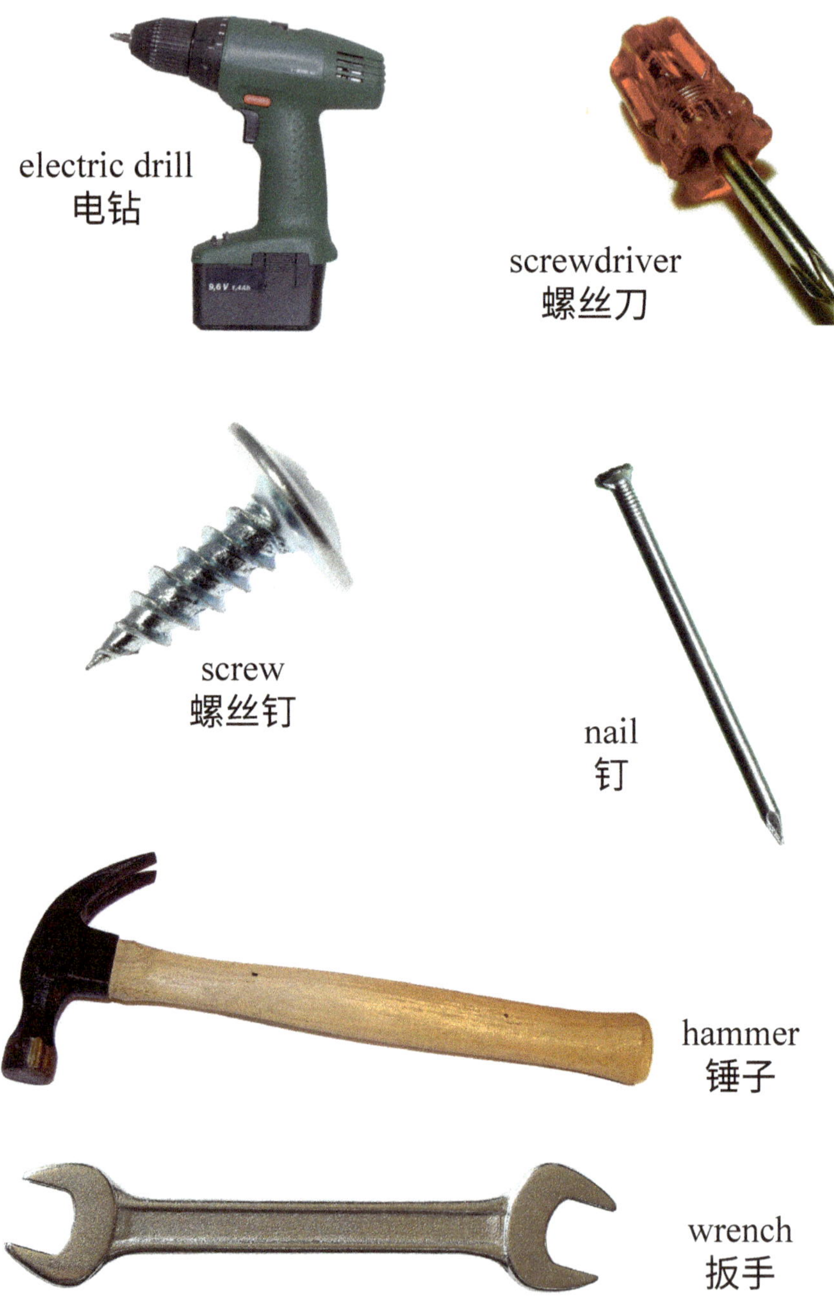
electric drill
电钻
screwdriver
螺丝刀
screw
螺丝钉
nail
钉
hammer
锤子
wrench
扳手

credit card
信用卡

wallet
钱包

banknote
钞票

coin
硬币

timetable
时间表

passport
护照

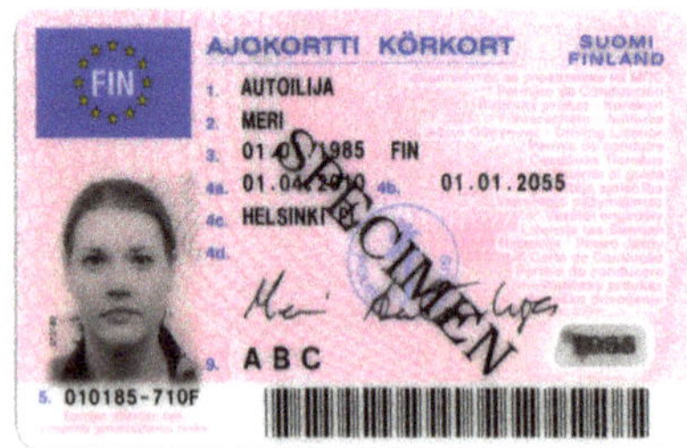

driving licence
驾驶执照

fingerprint
指纹

violin
小提琴

saxophone
萨克斯风

drum
鼓

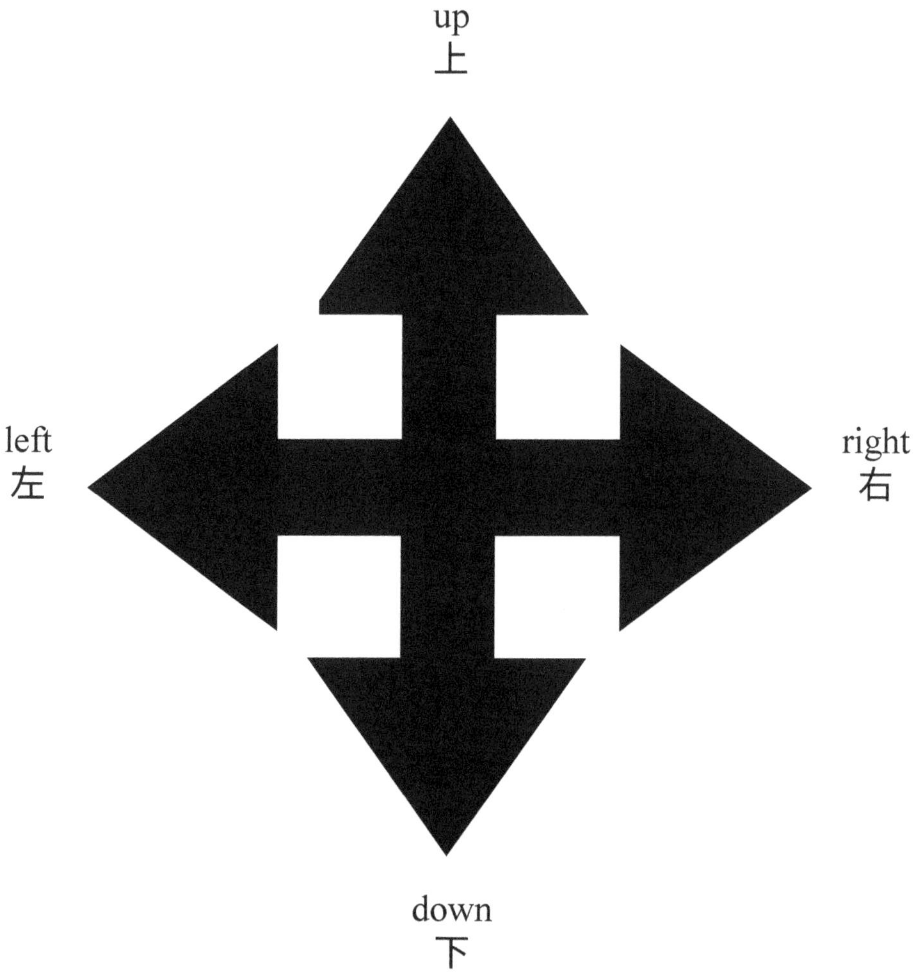
up
上
left
左
right
右
down
下

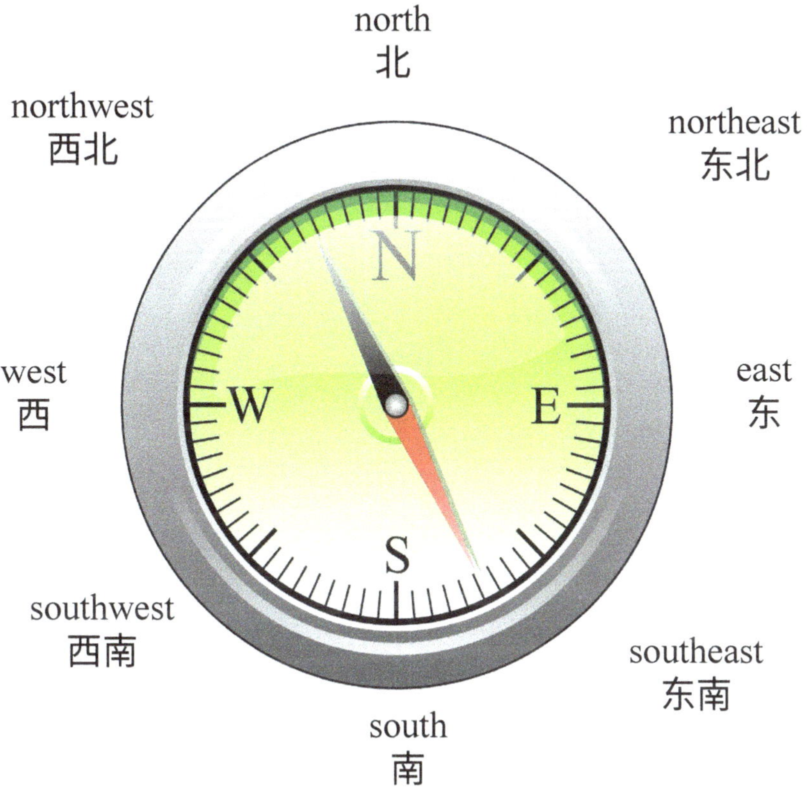

north
北
northwest
西北
northeast
东北
west
西
east
东
N
W
E
S
southwest
西南
southeast
东南
south
南

shoulder bag
单肩包

briefcase
公文包

plastic bag
塑料袋

backpack
背包

pen
笔
pencil
铅笔
ruler
尺子
notebook
笔记本
eraser
橡皮擦

car
车

bus
公交车

van
货车

train
火车

tram
电车

motorcycle
摩托车

bicycle
自行车

airplane
飞机

scooter
小型摩托车

ship
船

helicopter
直升机

truck
卡车

traffic lights
红绿灯

traffic sign
交通标志

zebra crossing
斑马线

gas station
加油站

bus stop
公交车站

vacuum cleaner
吸尘器

dishwasher
洗碗机

mop
拖把

smoothing iron
熨斗

washing machine
洗衣机

ironing board
烫衣板

dish brush
洗碗刷

cleaning sponge
清洁海绵

cleaning cloth
清洁布

dusting pan
垃圾铲

broom
扫帚

spray bottle
喷雾瓶

bucket
水桶

cot
婴儿床

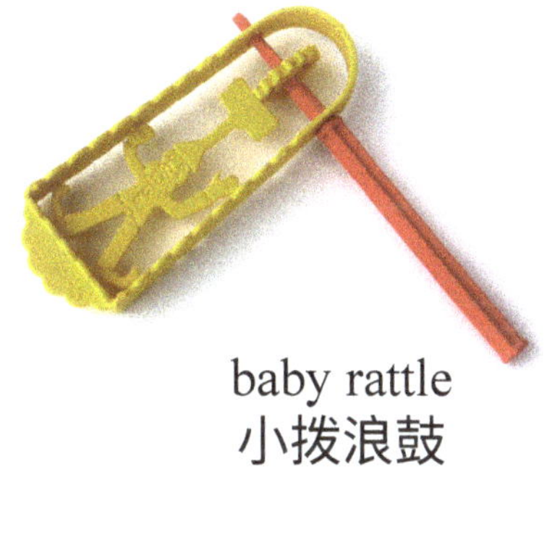

baby rattle
小拨浪鼓

diaper
尿布

pacifier
奶嘴

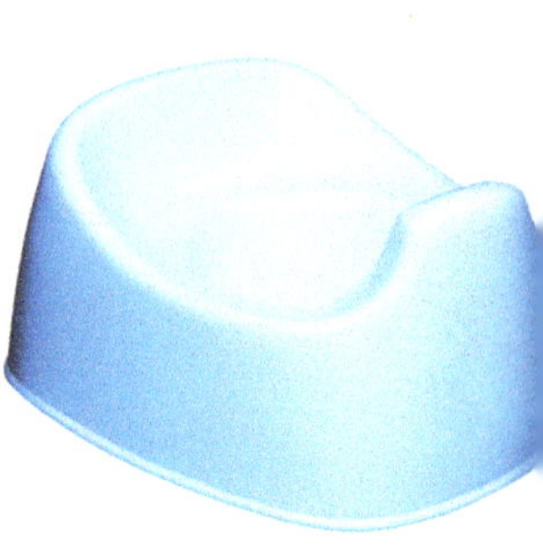

potty
便壶

pram
婴儿车

baby bottle
婴儿奶瓶

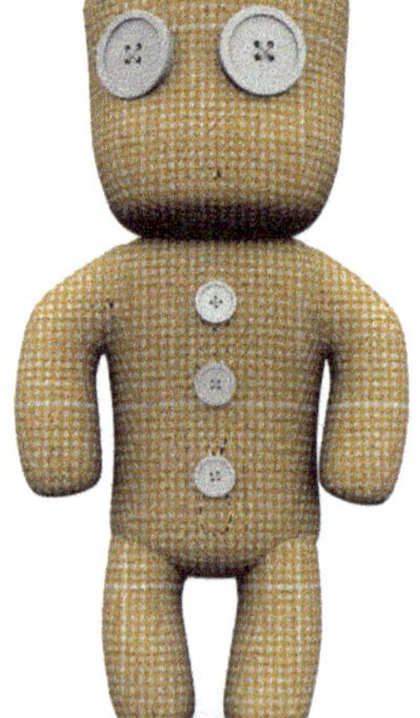

doll
娃娃

football
足球

kite
风筝

dice
骰子

game console
游戏机

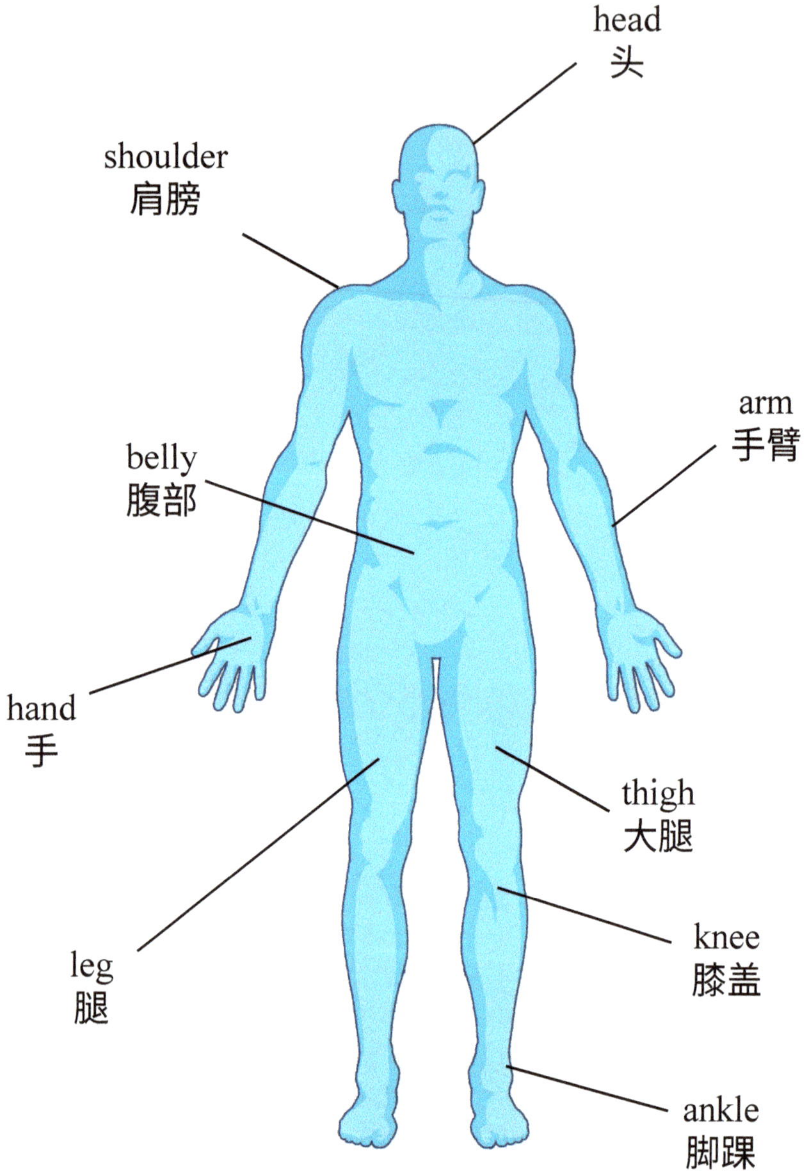
head
头
shoulder
肩膀
arm
手臂
belly
腹部
hand
手
thigh
大腿
leg
腿
knee
膝盖
ankle
脚踝

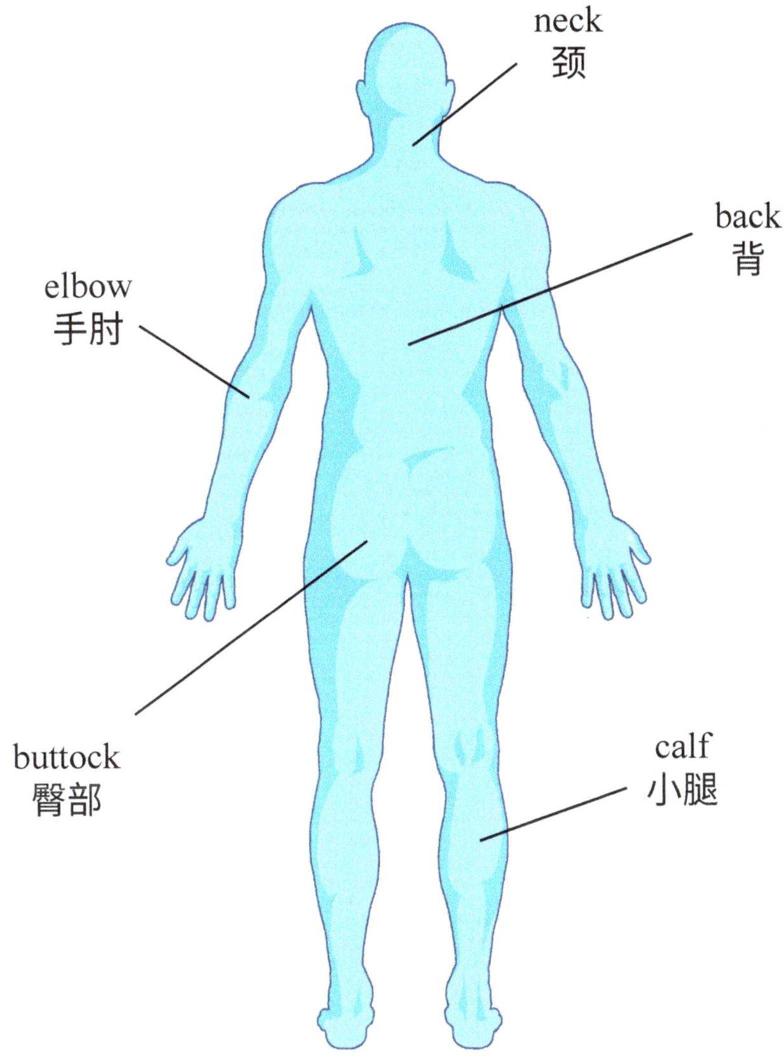

neck
颈
back
背
elbow
手肘
buttock
臀部
calf
小腿

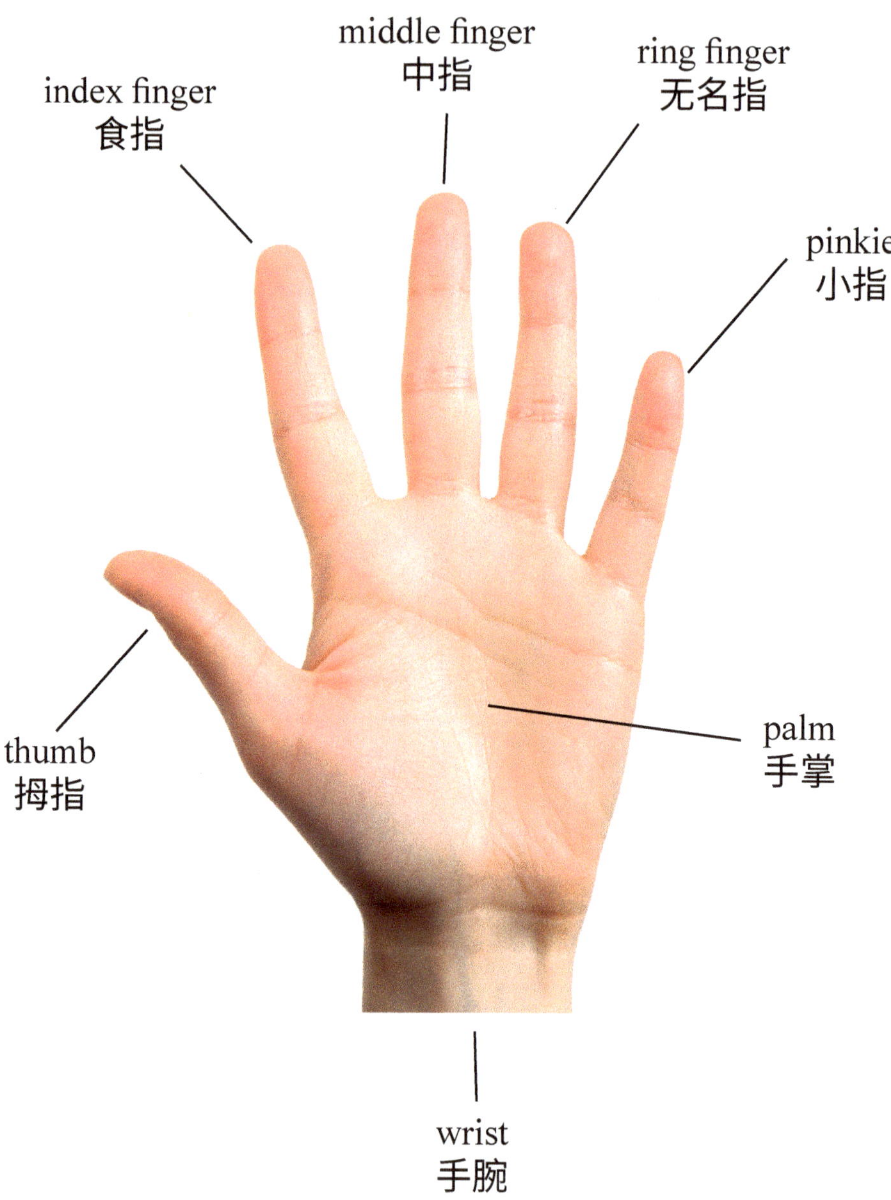

middle finger
中指
ring finger
无名指
index finger
食指
pinkie
小指
thumb
拇指
palm
手掌
wrist
手腕

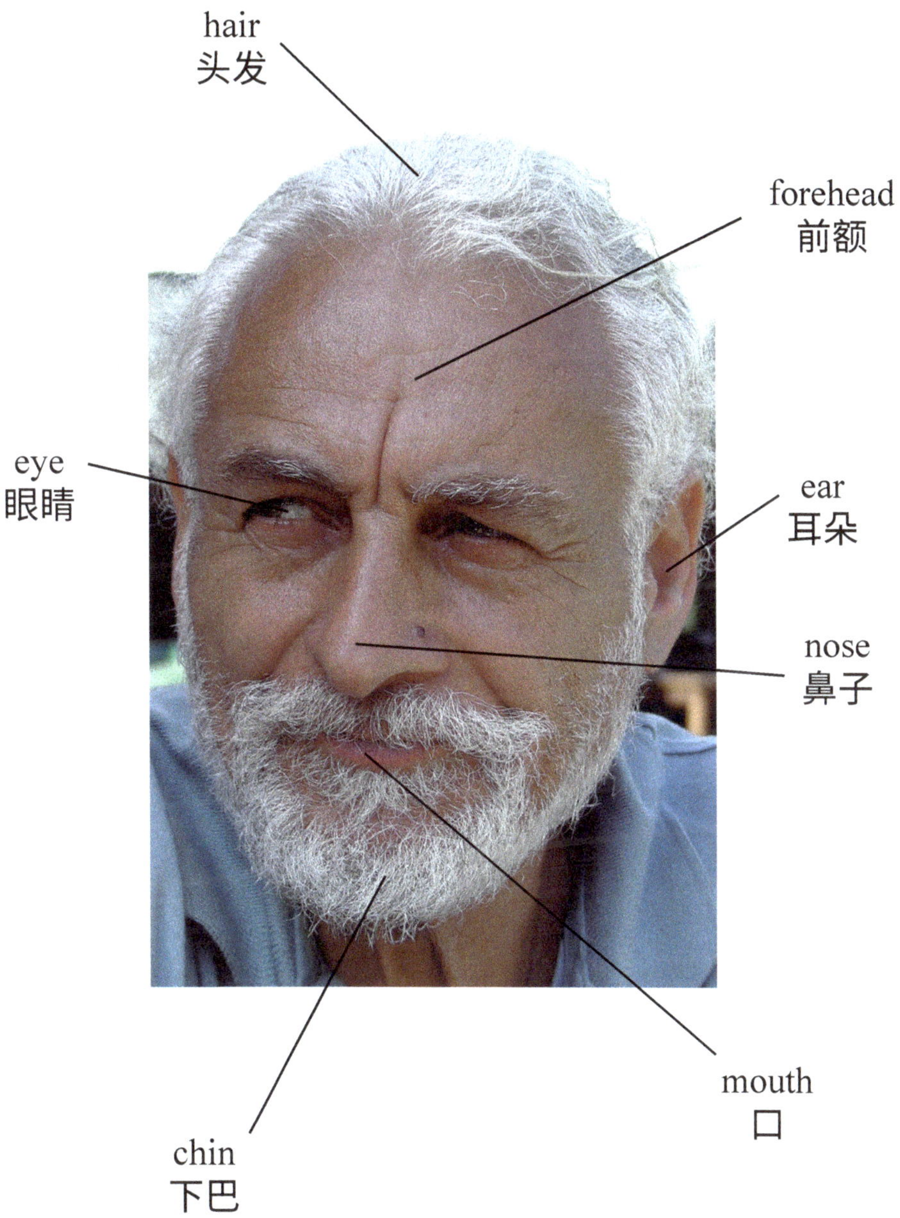

hair
头发
forehead
前额
eye
眼睛
ear
耳朵
nose
鼻子
mouth
口
chin
下巴

pharmacy
药店

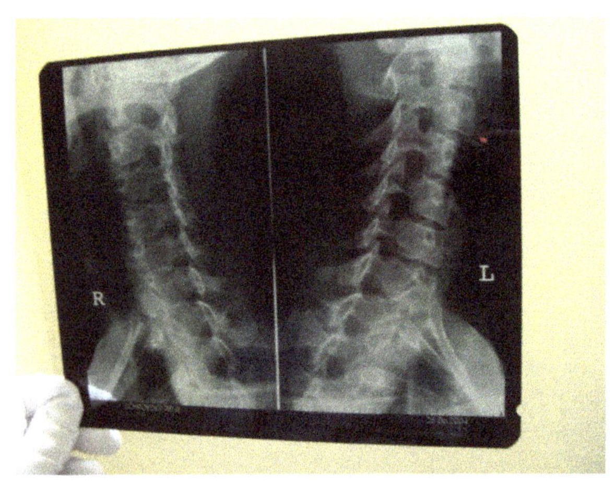

x-ray image
X射线图像

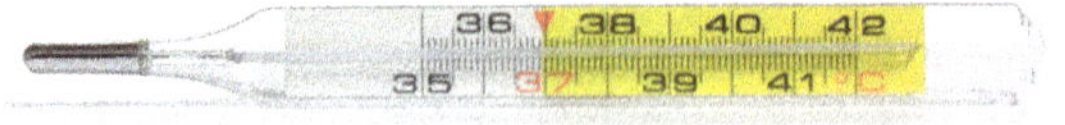

thermometer
体温计

ambulance
救护车

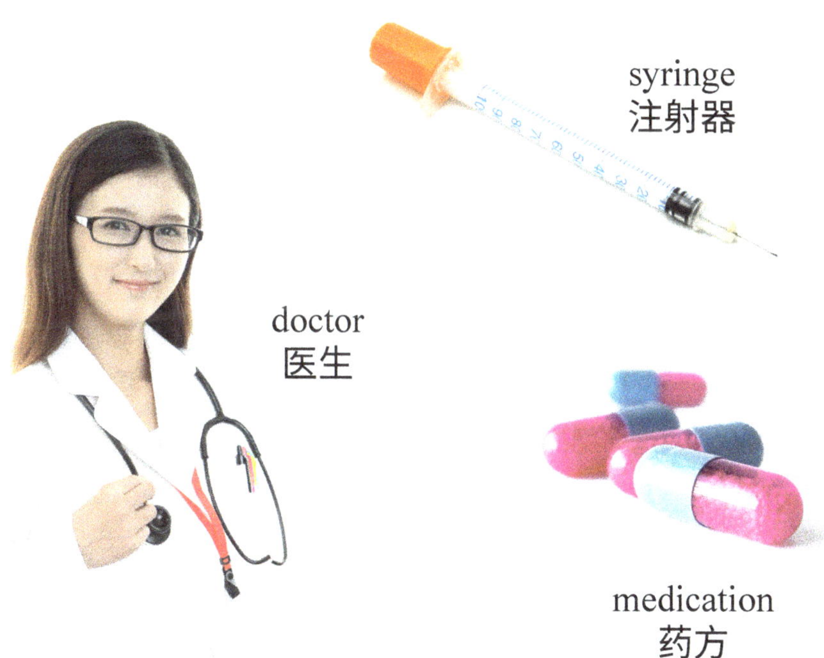

syringe
注射器

doctor
医生

medication
药方

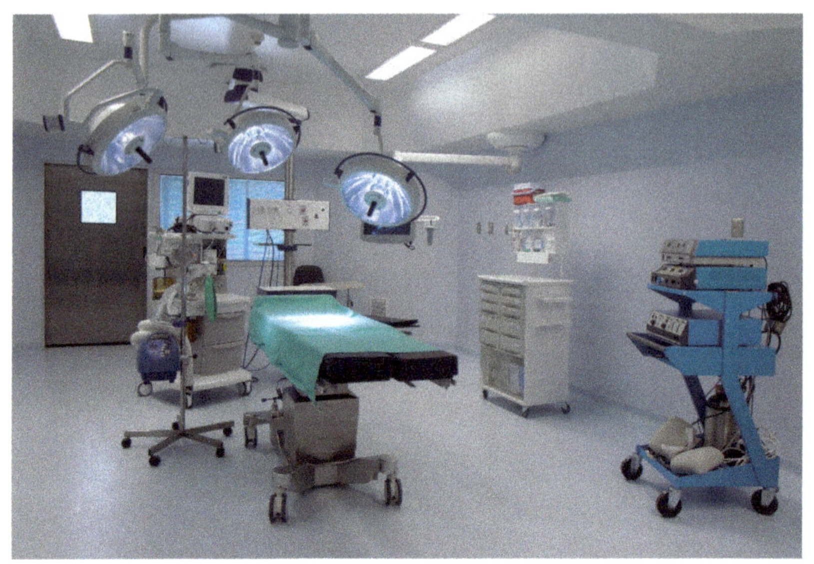

operating room
手术室

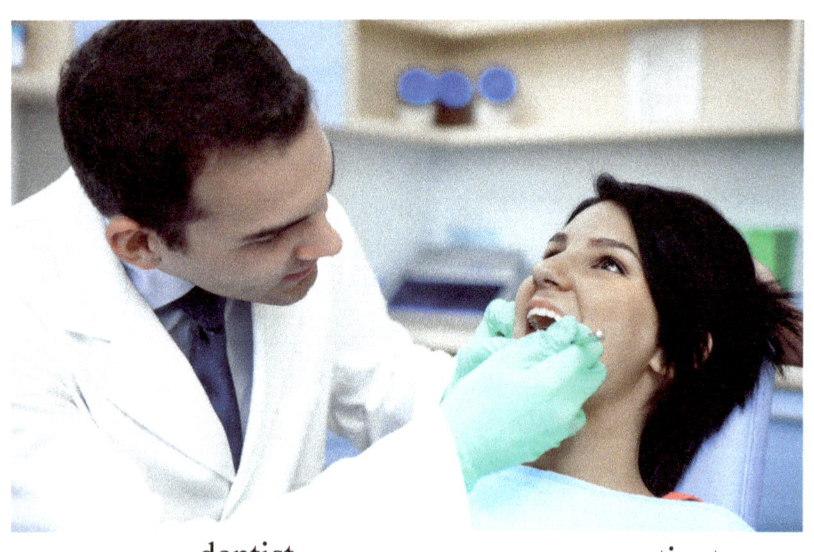

dentist
牙医

patient
患者

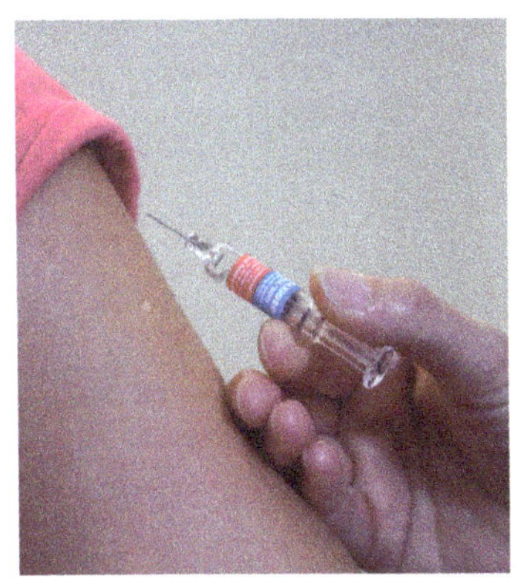

vaccination
接种疫苗

hospital
医院

band aid
创可贴

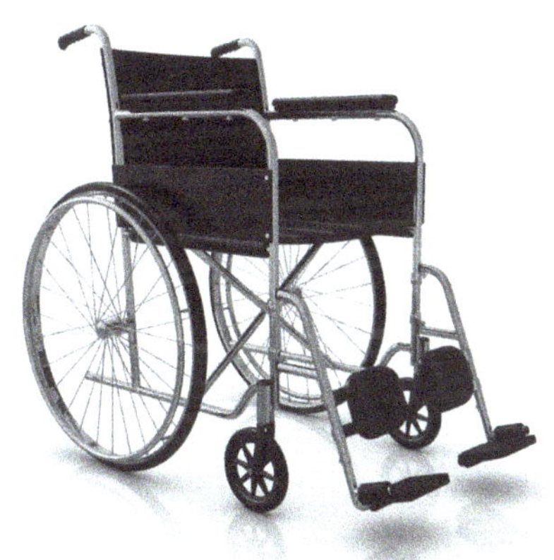

wheelchair
轮椅

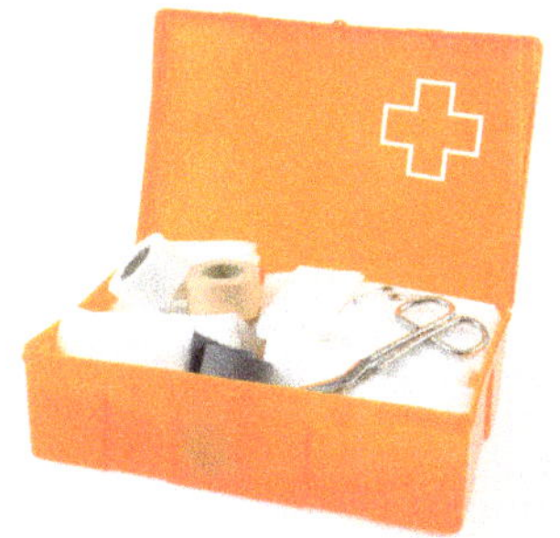

first aid kit
急救箱

to eat
吃

to drink
喝

to walk
走

to sit
坐

to talk
说话

to laugh
笑

to carry
携带

to stand
站立

to smile
微笑

to clean
清洁

to cook
做饭

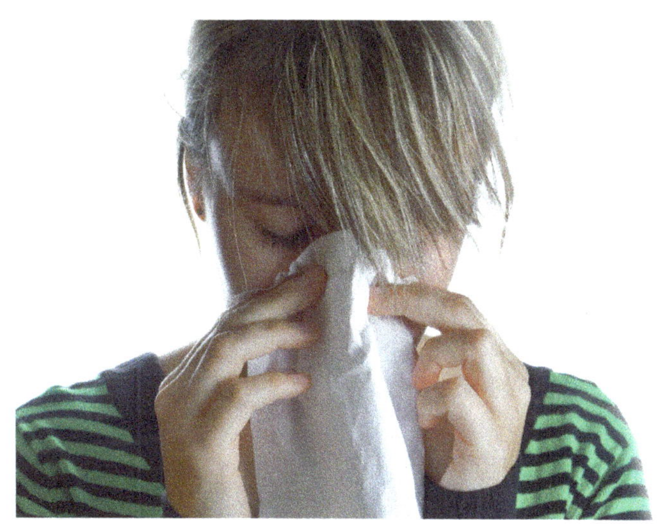

to sneeze
打喷嚏

to cry
哭

to hug
拥抱

to sleep
睡觉

to jump
跳

to run
跑步

to swim
游泳

to read
阅读

to teach
教

to play
玩

to write
写

square
正方形

triangle
三角形

rectangle
长方形

circle
圆圈

ellipse
椭圆

black
黑色
blue
蓝色
yellow
黄色
white
白色
green
绿色
gray
灰色
red
红色
brown
棕色

happy
快乐

angry
愤怒

uncertain
不确定

surprised
惊讶

confused
困惑

supportive
支持

thoughtful
周到

doubtful
疑惑

big
大

small
小

fast
快

slow
慢

good
好

bad
坏

light
轻

heavy
重

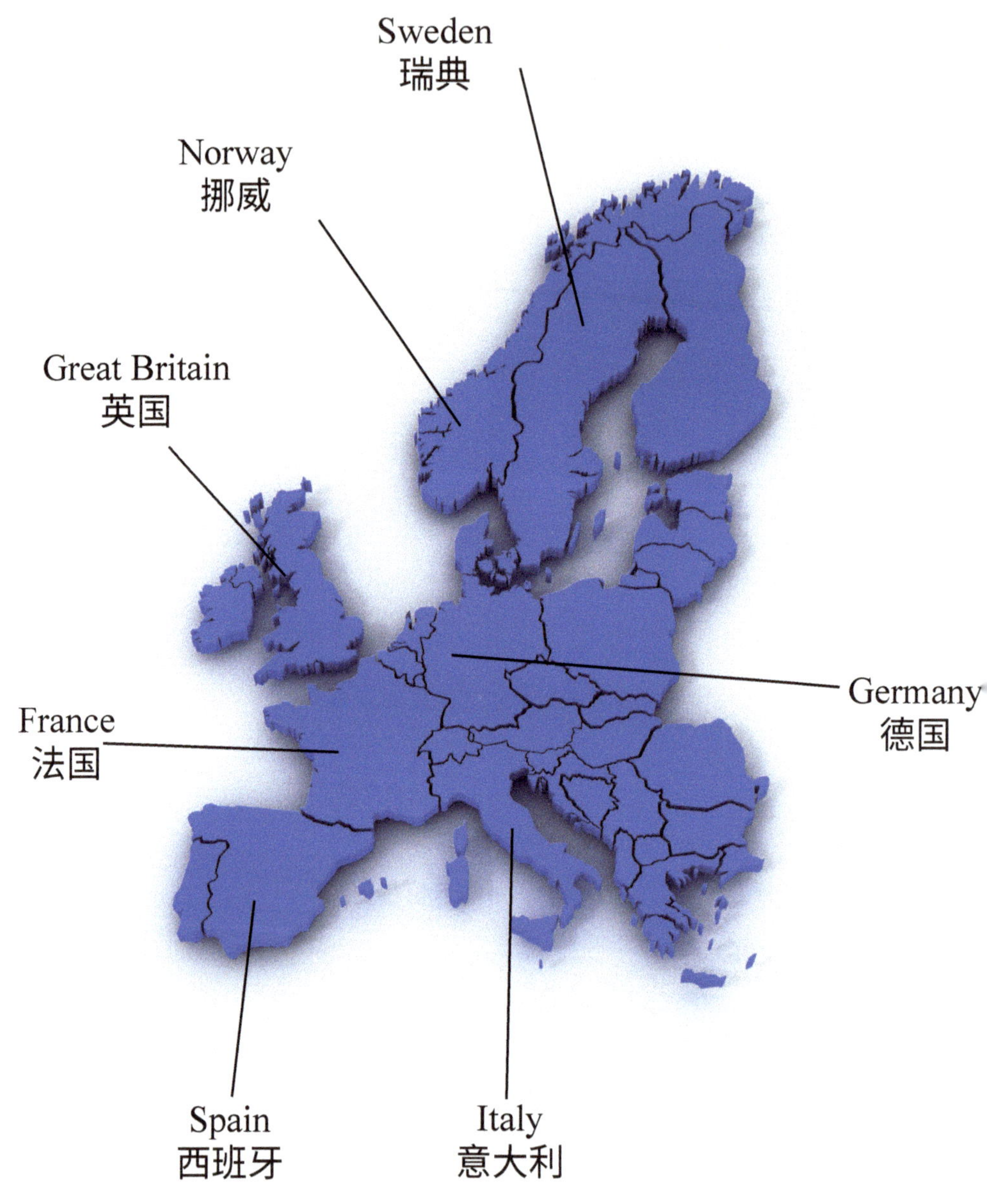

Sweden
瑞典
Norway
挪威
Great Britain
英国
Germany
德国
France
法国
Spain
西班牙
Italy
意大利

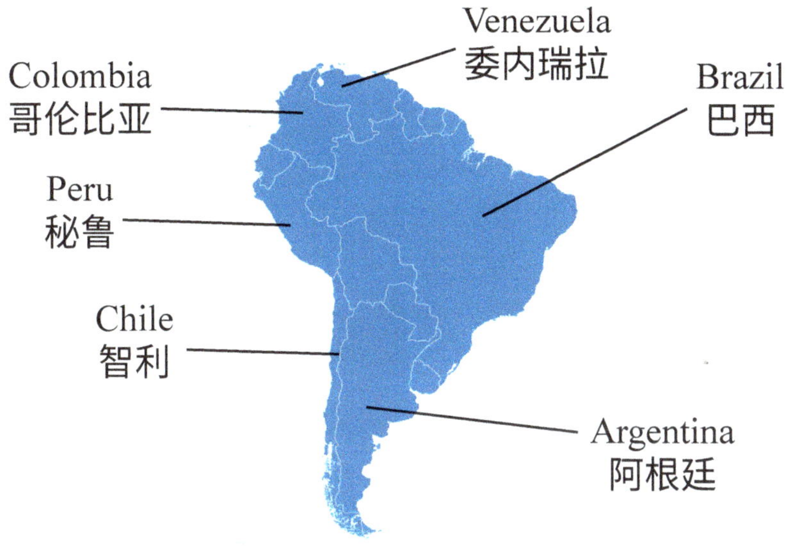

Colombia
哥伦比亚
Venezuela
委内瑞拉
Brazil
巴西
Peru
秘鲁
Chile
智利
Argentina
阿根廷

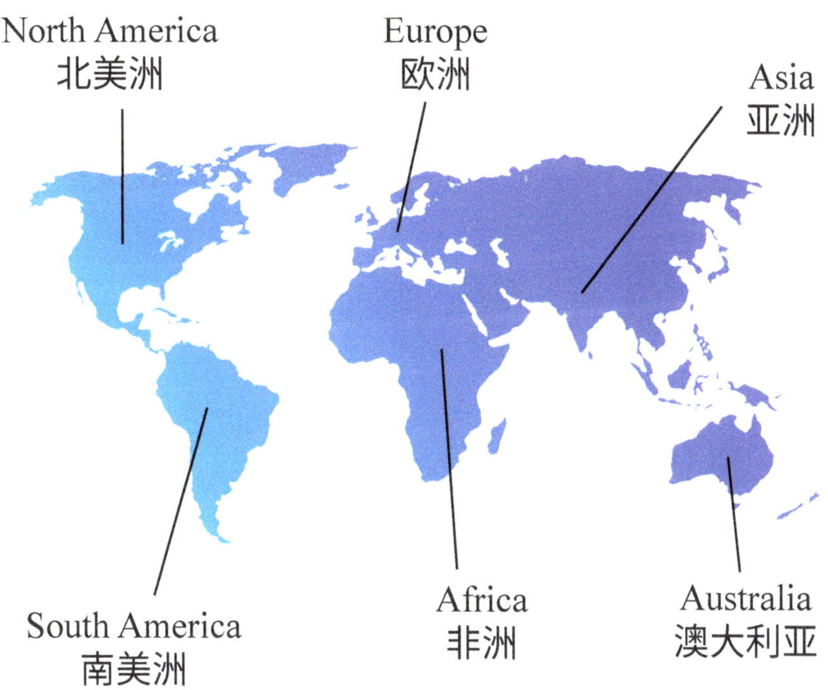

North America
北美洲
Europe
欧洲
Asia
亚洲
South America
南美洲
Africa
非洲
Australia
澳大利亚

spring
春天

summer
夏天

autumn
秋天

winter
冬天

hairdresser
美发师

florist
花匠

cleaner
清洁工人

chef
厨师

waitress
女服务员

musician
音乐家
guitar
吉他
loudspeaker
玻璃罐

microphone
麦克风
reporter
记者

teacher

老师

9 789518 771459